ABC in Boston

All 'Bout Cities

Murray Hill Books LLC
www.murrayhillbooks.com

Aa

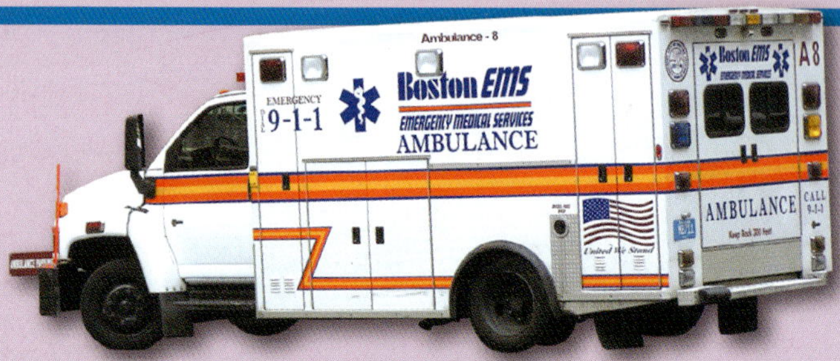

ambulance

apartment building

alley

airplanes

Bb

Bunker Hill Monument

baked beans

bus

Beacon Hill

bicycles

Cc

clam chowder

Boston Common

City Hall

cobblestones

Copley Square

Charlie Ticket

clock

Charles River

Customs
House
tower

Dd

dumpsters

duckling statues

ducks

deliveryman

Downtown Crossing

Ee

elevator

Esplanade

Ff

flowers

flag

fish and chips

fall foliage

Faneuil Hall

firefighters

fire engine

Fenway Park

Gg

geese

graffiti

green line

hamburge

Haymarket

Hh

horse and carriage

hip hop dancers

Harvard Bridge

Ii

Inner Harbor

Italian ices

Institute of Contemporary Art

Jj

John Hancock Tower

joggers

Kk

kids

kayakers

license plate

leaves

Ll

lagoon

Longfellow Bridge

lobsters

library

Mm

map of Boston

manhole covers

musician

meter

Massachusetts State House

mailbox

marina

Nn

newspaper distributor

North End

onlookers

Old Ironsides

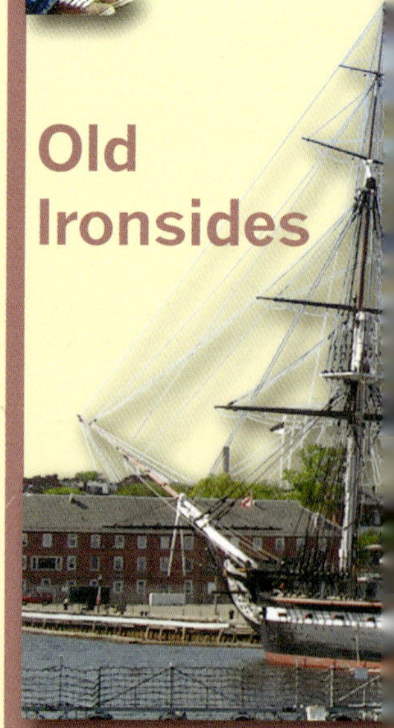

Oo

Old State House

Old South Church

Pp

Paul Revere House

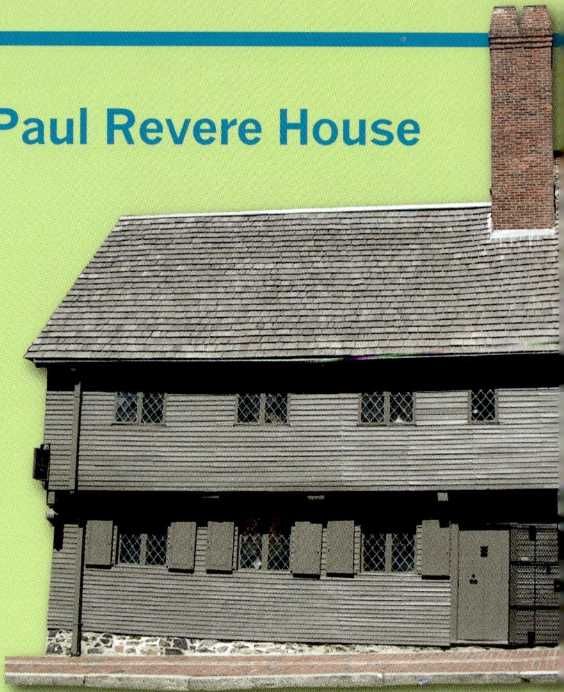

patrol car

police officers

payphones

pigeons

Prudential Tower

Public Garden

picnic table

police barriers

Qq

Quincy Market

rollerbladers

Rr

reflecting pool

rowers

ramp

Ss

sailboats

swan boat

street signs

Symphony Hall

souvenir shirt seller

Storrow Drive

squirrel

South Station

Tt

tree

Trinity Church

trash can

taxi

tourists

T tracks

T sign

traffic light

tour bus

tugboats

Uu

umbrellas

Vv

vegetable
vendors

violinist

Ww

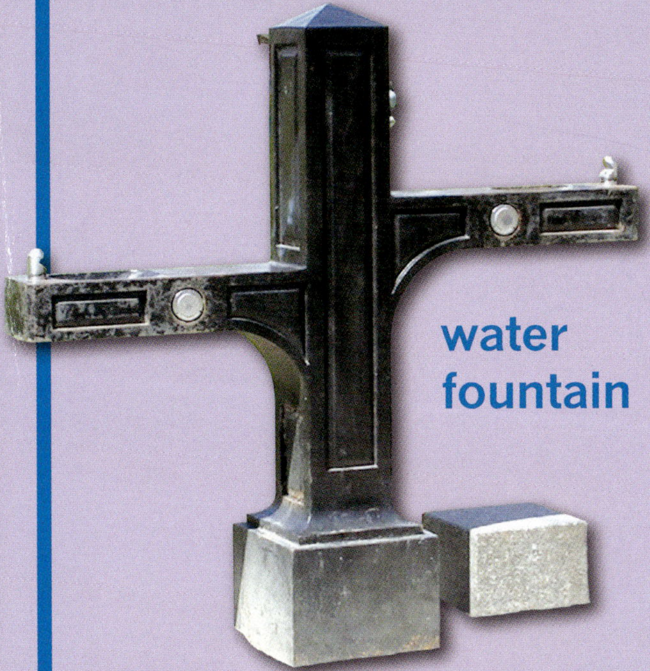

water fountain

walk signal button

walk signal

World Trade Center

Xx

xing
(crossing)

Yy

yellow cab

Zz

Zakim Bunker Hill Bridge

Murray Hill Books, LLC
P.O. Box 4393
New York, NY 10163

www.murrayhillbooks.com
info@murrayhillbooks.com
SAN 256-3622

Library of Congress Control Number: 2008902558
ISBN: 9780971969711

Photography, Design, and Editing by Robin Segal. Additional photographic editing by Wei Lieh Lee, Samantha Cohn, and Ilyse Segal.